SILENCE IS
YOUR
SUPERPOWER

Illustrations by TUBC

Second Edition: 2024

Dedication

I dedicate this book to my amazing Mumma Bear. I wish you were here to pretend to read it and tell me how proud you are of me.

To my wonderful son Harry, to whom I also dedicate every grey hair I have.

To my best friend, Lisa, for being my biggest cheerleader and being with me on every step of this journey.

To my family, but especially my nephew Tom who gave me the inspiration even to start this book.

Lastly, I dedicate this to you, the heartbroken person reading this—you are not alone, my darling!

CONTENTS

About the Author

Meet Kellie, the author of:

- *Silence is Your Superpower*

- *Day No Contact Diary (an accompaniment to Silence is Your Superpower)*

- *Bossing Your Breakup ... and*

- *Men. WTF?*

Kellie is 'The Ultimate Breakup Coach' who is transforming lives, one heartbreak at a time.

Hailing from the vibrant city of London, Kellie shares her home with Max, a scruffy, white 14-year-old dog who has been her loyal companion through thick and thin. Kellie's journey has been one marked with lots of amazing experiences, but also personal heartbreaks It's these experiences that have shaped her into the popular, empathetic and skilled breakup coach she is today.

Kellie's passion for reading and writing has been a lifelong journey. This passion, combined with her personal experiences, inspired her to write books to help put the advice into practice. Silence is Your Superpower is a guide designed to help those navigating the challenging path of heartbreak or needing to get their ex back. This book offers practical strategies and support, empowering readers to harness their inner strength and create a fulfilling life post-breakup.

In addition to being an author and a breakup coach, Kellie loves spending time with her friends and family. Whether it's a quiet moment with a captivating book or a lively gathering with loved ones, she cherishes these moments more than anything.

Kellie's mission as a breakup coach extends beyond her one-on-one sessions. Through her books, she reaches out to individuals worldwide, providing them with the tools and guidance they need to turn their pain into power.

Her compassionate approach coupled with tons of research & her first-hand experience coaching many clients from all walks of life, offers a comforting and supportive space for readers and clients alike, helping them to not just survive, but thrive after a breakup.

So, if you're grappling with heartbreak and seeking a path to healing, Kellie's books offer a lifeline. With her expertise, personal understanding, and Max's loyal companionship, Kellie is here to guide you towards resilience and a future filled with love and happiness.

INTRODUCTION

"Creating Your Superpower"

Breakups are bloody hard ...

I have been where you are right now, so I know it's a tough and lonely place.

Before we get into it, let me tell you a bit about myself. I had always considered myself to be a very positive person who never let life get her down, but when life threw me a few curve balls in quick succession - a breakup when I discovered my boyfriend was cheating, the loss of my darling dad, and my mum having a stroke. Times were hard.

I was left heartbroken and lost, and I believed I was totally worthless. I had no idea who I was anymore or what I wanted out of life, and I felt completely scared and overwhelmed. I felt useless as a parent, a friend, and at work. I struggled to eat or sleep.

I spent the next year (yes, YEAR) in a massive tailspin, endlessly scouring the internet for ways to make myself feel better. However, I did not commit to practising the techniques I was reading about, preferring to read about them rather than doing the work.

Nothing changed, and I felt no one understood what I was going through. I know I was annoying my friends and family by constantly going over the same things about my ex, time and time again. I would see the look on their faces when I spoke about the breakup yet again, which made me feel even worse. They didn't understand why I wasn't 'over it already'.

It wasn't until I caved in and signed up with a Breakup Coach that I realised how common my feelings were and what I was going through. That was a light bulb moment, as I swear, I believed I was the only one ever to feel this way! Or if others had felt heartbreak, they had never quite as bad as how I felt.

So, I decided I needed help …

I bit the bullet and hired an amazing coach who created a non-judgmental, safe space where I felt supported and encouraged as I worked through my issues, tackling my pain at the source and enabling my healing journey to begin truly.

With the help of my coach, I rebuilt my confidence - gaining an unwavering belief in myself along the way – and I truly began living a happy, successful, and strong life that was of my OWN creation. After this experience, I knew I had to help others do the same, so that was why I became a breakup coach.

Today, I am committed to and passionate about helping people recover from break-ups and live their best lives. Anyway, enough about me, the real question is:

"How can I help you?"

Well, I will help you understand what is happening to you right now, let go of your past in a healthy way, and find the confidence you'll need to change your life so that you will not only survive your breakup but thrive because of it.

From healing your heart to winning back your ex, leaving your partner, and finding new love, I can help, as I've been there, done that, and worn the T-shirt! When I was going through breakups, I would find myself scouring the internet looking for the silver bullet that would take away this heartbreak and bring my ex back—the magic pill to remove the pain and know there's hope. Does that sound familiar?

In my quest to alleviate the excruciating pain that I was in. I came across many different resources. Lots of different advice, and it was all very conflicting and quite confusing. So, I decided to create a very simple-to-understand Book to help you with the best tip I was ever given when faced with a breakup that I did not want …. **NO CONTACT!!!**

It was literally life-changing! I promise you it was the only thing that got me through the pain. It works, but you *must* know how to do it correctly! Most people who say they are doing No Contact are not doing it right, so they think it does not work. It is not a manipulation game, and if you use it as such, you will be left very disappointed. You need to follow it to the letter.

In this book, I have simplified it for you, and I included real-life No Contact accounts so that you don't have to spend hours scouring for proof that this works, as I did.

I have bolded the most important parts, so take note of them!

CHAPTER 1

"So, what is this all about?"

Does this sound familiar? You two broke up. You went into shock mode, panicking, and began to chase, beg, plead, harass, phone, email, message, or stalk (okay, not all of them; just pick whichever one you did). Most of us will likely do some (or all) of these things during this stage. To top it off, then:

- You lose weight.
- You neglect yourself, your house, and your job (hours spent scouring the internet looking for the magic pill to take the pain away).
- You drive your friends and family crazy talking about the breakup.
- You cry at the drop of a hat.
- You feel like a zombie.
- You can't even comprehend that your life might not include your ex again.
- You begin putting them on a pedestal, forgetting all the nagging things about them that used to drive you crazy. In your mind, they have become 'perfect'.
- You convince yourself that you're a total loser who just ruined a relationship with "the best person in the world." You KNOW without a doubt that you'll never EVER love like that again.
- You know no one else will come along who is even close to being as amazing as your ex.
- You wear a sad face for the world to see. (You should see my passport picture taken two days after my breakup; it's just pitiful.)

So, you may have heard about the infamous 'No Contact' rule, but you have no clue what it's all about or how to use it effectively to get your ex back. Then you came across this book.

Hang on, before we get into it, let me answer a few questions you may have:

"What is no contact (NC)?"

No contact is just that—it's breaking all ties with your ex. It is done after you've been dumped or are going through a breakup that was instigated by your partner, and you don't want the breakup.

"What is NC used for?"

In brief, no contact is the best and quickest way for you to heal and move on. It gives you time to breathe and take stock of the situation. Being dumped is a big shock and can make you cry and beg your ex back (the worst thing to do).

"Will NC get my ex back?"

No Contact (NC) isn't some magical voodoo to manipulate your ex back into your life. Sure, absence can make the heart grow fonder, but relying on NC as a manipulation tactic? You're only setting yourself up for disappointment.

The purpose of NC isn't to play mind games or force someone's hand. It's about giving yourself the time and space to heal, reflect, and grow after a breakup. It's about reclaiming your power and self-worth, not scheming to get your ex back at any cost.

I understand that breakups are tough, and the idea of your ex missing you and realising what they've lost can be tempting. But true love and healthy relationships aren't built on manipulation or desperation. They're built on mutual respect, trust, and a genuine desire to be together.

So, instead of obsessing over your ex and trying to force something that might not be meant to be, use the time in NC to focus on yourself. Use this time to rediscover your passions, surround yourself with loved ones, and work on becoming the best version of yourself. Who knows? Maybe your ex will come around and miss you. Or maybe you'll realise that you deserve someone who appreciates you for who you are, without any games or manipulation.

Trust the process, and let NC do its thing – not as a ploy, but as a path to healing and self-love.

"What should I be doing during NC?"

First things first, let's give that grieving process the space it needs to unfold naturally. Grieving a loss is essential, but dwelling on it won't do you any favours. Instead, surround yourself with your fabulous friends and family, dive into a new hobby that excites you, get those endorphins pumping with a killer workout routine, or start building that business you dream of.

But listen, I get it—sometimes, we all need a little extra support on this journey. That's where coaching can be an absolute lifesaver. My Breakup Coach was an absolute godsend when I was feeling broken and lost. They provided a totally nonjudgmental, unbiased space for me to work through my stuff. A good coach is like having your very own cheerleader and fairy godmother all rolled into one!

So, if you're feeling stuck or like you could use a little extra guidance, don't be shy! You can easily find me at www.kelscoaching.com.

"Will NC make my Ex forget about me?"

They will 100% NOT forget you!

No contact will make them think of you more, not less. If you're not there begging and pleading, you'll, by default, become more attractive to them. If there's even a glimmer of hope for getting back together, your best bet is always to take a step back, give them some space, and focus on yourself for a bit.

"My ex wants to be friends, should I?"

No, not, especially if you are still in love with them. For the most part, exes will want to keep you as a friend, so they have a 'backup plan' in case things fail with the new love of their life. Ask yourself if you're happy being second in someone's life. If so, that is your choice. But if you respect yourself and have healthy self-esteem, you'll never settle for being left hanging on a string.

Furthermore, keeping you as a 'friend' is designed to make THEM feel better about things - not you. Keeping you as a friend is a way of relieving their guilt and convincing themselves that it can't hurt all that much if you're willing to just be a buddy, right?

Wrong.

Breakups are hard enough without your ex adding salt to the wound by demanding an instant friendship. Take all the time you need to heal; it's so important. Don't let anyone, especially the person who broke your heart, pressure you into something you're not ready for. Your emotional well-being comes first, always.

My advice? Unless you have the emotional fortitude of a Buddhist monk, politely decline that 'friend' nonsense, and take some time to value yourself. You are not a pigeon, and you deserve more than breadcrumbs!

So, in answer to this question, do not agree to stay as friends - it will prolong the pain and cement the agony.

"I can't resist the urge to contact my ex! What do I do??"

You've deleted their number, but deep down, you still know how to reach out, don't you? Ah, but here's the thing: instead of giving in to that temptation, why not give your bestie a ring? Better yet, get those endorphins pumping by hitting the gym, going for a cheeky bike ride, or even a brisk jog around the park. Anything to keep your mind occupied and away from that ex of yours.

Let's be real. They're probably out living their best lives, not sitting around waiting for your call. So do yourself a favour, get out there, and focus on yourself for a change. That's the way to move on and truly find your happiness again.

Exercise releases endorphins: after a while, the more you take care of yourself, the better you'll look. And the better you look, the better you'll feel. Win-win!

"How long should I wait to contact my ex?"

You wait until there is snow in the Sahara Desert!! You simply don't! If they dumped you, it is their responsibility to realise and make amends. Stand firm.

"What happens if I cave in and break NC?"

You'll end up right back at square one and must start all over. Trust me, while you are in NC with them, and they are with someone else, you don't want to know how they're doing or hear how happy they are. If you're nursing a shattered heart, you can't handle what they have to say.

Why rip out the stitches and tear the wound open again? If you pass razor wire up one nostril and down the other while poking your eyes out with needles - it will hurt only marginally less than talking to them and getting nothing from them but pain.

A question I get asked a lot is, 'What about birthdays?' Yeah, right. What about them? They are just another day, just another situation to ignore completely and utterly. Do not ever send any form of birthday wish (just another excuse to cling to them), and do not respond to anything they send you (just more breadcrumbs rubbish).

"What if I bump into my ex in public?"

Bottom line: Avoid contact with them at all costs. If you can't, just be polite, smile, and wave if they wave at you. If they want to talk, remember the rule: no small talk, no information, make your excuses and leave the situation (being late for an appointment comes to mind). As far as they're concerned, it should really look as if you're doing great without them – even if you aren't.

"What if my Ex never contacts me?"

Then, it was never meant to be. Consider yourself lucky and smart enough to realise that. The sooner you implement No Contact and get on with your life, the sooner you can feel happy again and maybe even meet the right person for you. That's really what this whole 'no-contact' deal is all about healing and moving on.

"What do I do if I have obligations with my ex that make Complete No Contact impossible?"

Well, I suppose we're discussing the care of children, the

legal division of property, or the professional requirements of having to work together, aren't we? These are situations where you cannot avoid speaking to them at some point.

There is something you can do, though:

It's called 'LC' - Limited Contact and I discuss this later on in this book.

"What is the best way to get closure from my ex?"

The truth is that you will never, ever get closure directly from your ex. The person who broke you cannot fix you.

Any answers or responses you get will simply prompt more questions from you. Because deep down, all you want from closure is for them to do an about-turn and admit they were wrong. You want them to change their minds. Seeking closure just reeks of desperation, and it will merely serve to break your heart again.

1. Very often, they themselves may be confused about the situation, so you may get one answer one day and a different one the next...
2. They might lie, either to protect themselves or to protect your feelings. This, of course, is pointless because your feelings are shattered anyway.
3. Any answers or responses you get will simply prompt more questions from you. Because deep down, all you want from closure is for them to do an about-turn and admit they were wrong. You want them to change their minds. Seeking closure just

reeks of desperation, and it will merely serve to break your heart again.

Listen, this is not one size fits all. Every breakup is different and warrants a different level of no contact, but the rule of thumb is that you should no longer rely on your ex as a source of communication, comfort, or affection during this time.

People have been known to use a no-contact rule to get back together after a breakup. For years, people have believed that cutting off contact with a former partner after a breakup can make them realise their mistakes and bring them back.

"I heard that No Contact would work to get my ex back?"

No contact is the consequence of a breakup that you did not want. Your ex has said they want you out of their life, so that is exactly what you should do. Give them the breakup they asked for.

The no-contact rule can successfully get an ex back after a breakup because it removes you from the spotlight and prevents them from raising their defences against you. You see while using the No-Contact rule, you're not begging or pleading for them to take you back. They are not having to fight against getting back together with you; they are not reinforcing their reasons in their own minds for breaking up with you day after day. This can make them see you differently.

CHAPTER 2

"How to deal with the breakup?"

Let me share a little wisdom with you. Instead of engaging in a tug-of-war with your ex when they break up with you, the smartest move is to stop begging them to reconsider. Take a step back and give them some space using the No Contact approach.

By not constantly hounding them or trying to force a reconciliation, you're increasing the chances of them reconsidering the situation with a clearer mind. It's like taking a breather from an intense argument—it allows both parties to cool off and potentially see things from a new perspective.

Let's be real here: Fighting against the breakup is only going to make you come across as their opponent, which is the last thing you want. You don't want to be seen as the enemy, do you? Instead, by gracefully accepting the situation (as difficult as it may be), you're not only preserving your dignity but also leaving the door open for a potential reconciliation down the line.

So, while it may seem counter-intuitive, sometimes the best way to handle a breakup is to give your ex the space they desire. Trust me, this approach has a way of making them realise what they're missing, and who knows? They might just miss you and return to you with a newfound appreciation and a willingness to work things out. I know it's tough, but sometimes a little distance can do wonders for rekindling that lost spark, you know?

In other words, your ex won't be so focused on fighting for

the breakup and for you to leave them alone that they forget what they were fighting for. If you are in no contact, they can see the true consequences of their actions and might decide that they don't want to be broken up.

No contact also allows your ex the opportunity to miss you.

Spoiler Alert The only way your ex can miss you is if you're not around them and not contacting them. What's more, No Contact allows your ex to see that you're capable of staying away from them, being without them, and ultimately, moving on. Your ex's belief that you're strong enough to move on and that they could lose you is crucial to their wanting to get back together with you.

It's when your stock price goes up and your ex stops expecting you to reach out to them that they feel the pressure to act to get you back, or else they realise that they risk losing you forever.

"How does my ex feel after they broke up with me?"

Well, immediately following the breakup, your ex is relieved because they've got such a difficult task over with. This breakup was not something they had just thought of; they had been thinking about it for a while. So, while it is a shock to you, it is not to them. The sooner you go into no-contact, the sooner their relief is over and the sooner the consequences of their actions set in. This is because right after the breakup, your ex assumes that they can get you back anytime they want you – if they were to want you again.

This is because they were the ones who initiated the breakup. They feel that since they wanted to end the relationship and you wanted to save it, they have all the power and that they are the prize you were unable to keep. However, when you don't chase them but rather utilise the no-contact rule, they very soon begin to feel the opposite.

They may begin to feel that you are out of reach and untouchable. They may start to wonder what you are doing or if you have met someone else. Then, they may start to feel they have made a mistake by giving up on you. They could then become concerned that they might not be able to get you back.

This is the power of the no-contact rule and what can ultimately attract your ex back to you.

However (take note … this is important), they may just be glad it's over and feel none of the above. So, using the No Contact rule solely to get them back is NOT a game you should play, and you should also never ever use this rule to get your revenge or to manipulate your ex.

The "no contact" approach is often touted as the best way to get your ex back, but I have to be real here. It's not some magical spell or love potion that will make them come running back to you against their will. That's just not how it works.

The truth is, the No Contact method can only work in your favour if your ex already has second thoughts about their decision to end things. Giving them space to miss you can be a game-changer if they're genuinely regretting the breakup and still have feelings for you. It allows them to reflect on what they've lost and potentially rekindle that spark.

But if your ex is certain about their decision and has moved on, well, no amount of radio silence will change their mind. At the end of the day, we can't force someone to love us, can we? As much as it hurts, sometimes we must accept that it's time to let go and focus on our own happiness.

So, while the No Contact approach can be useful, it's not a guaranteed way to get your ex back. It's about reading the signs and being honest with yourself about where your ex's heart truly lies. And if it's not with you, my love, then it's time to pick up the pieces and move on to someone who will appreciate the amazing person that you are!

While it's okay to hope that the relationship can be repaired once you both have time to work on your personal feelings, the No Contact rule should be about figuring out what you want, taking time to breathe, and calming down from the shock of the breakup.

If you play games and try to manipulate your former partner, then I can tell you categorically that you'll never know how they genuinely feel and if they're with you for the right reasons. You want them back, and you want it to work out, right? If so, then take the time in No Contact to truly work out what YOU feel, and then communicate with your ex if you still want to try again.

"So, what do I do after 30 days of no contact?"

This can be confusing. You've made it through the hardest days of the breakup, but now you must decide where to go from here. By asking yourself these questions after a 30-day no-contact period, you'll be able to figure out your next move:

- *How has my life changed (good & bad) without them in it?*
- *Am I feeling better than I did when we first broke up?*
- *Has my ex reached out or shown interest in reuniting?*
- *Has my ex moved on?*
- *Do I want them back for all the right reasons?*

Whether you reconcile with your ex or reconcile with your new, single self, it's okay. The fact is that by taking those 30 days to breathe, you will have begun to discover your true feelings, and you are moving on to a bigger, better, and brighter future (even though it might not feel this way right now)

Most people get the concept of the No Contact Rule all wrong.

Most people think the idea is that you won't contact your ex for a certain period (usually 30-60 days) before making contact again. However, this isn't how it goes. If your ex hasn't contacted you in that period (which is a long time), it means you're out, and initiating contact puts you in the same position as before.

When I say you're out, I mean the person who dumped you isn't missing you enough to call, so the chances are they're no longer in love with you (if they ever were). Therefore, any reason for getting back together after that period will be for a reason other than love - not good!

If done properly, the No Contact Rule always works!

Why?

Because, for better or for worse, it tells you exactly where you stand with that person.

CHAPTER 3

"How to implement this method correctly".

If you are the person who has been dumped, and it was not a breakup that you wanted and not a breakup that you caused by the mistreatment of your ex (abuse, cheating, etc)

Here's the best way to do it:

Break all contact and NEVER initiate it.

I know (first-hand) how tempting it can be to keep tabs on your ex but trust me, that's a path you don't want to go down. No calls, emails, texts—nada! Don't even think about stalking their social media or shared streaming accounts. Checking up on what they're watching on Netflix or scrolling through their Instagram feed is just going to reopen those wounds, and you've worked too hard to heal.

And please, for the love of all that's holy, don't start showing up at their yoga class or favourite coffee shop "by chance." That's just asking for a world of awkwardness and potential restraining orders! The healthiest thing you can do right now is to go full ghost mode. Vanish from their life completely, and in doing so, you'll find it much easier to make them disappear from yours, too.

I know it's tough, but you've got this! Rip off that band-aid, and soon enough, you'll be wondering why you ever wanted to keep tabs on them in the first place. Trust me, a life of freedom and new possibilities awaits when you finally let go.

In addition, get rid of their phone number, text messages, emails, and email addresses, and remove all the pictures, photos, memories, and gifts. Anything that reminds you of your ex should be boxed up and put in a safe place out of daily view and easy reach.

If necessary, get someone else to hold on to them for you. After a while, you won't know what's there, and you won't want it back, anyway. You also need to delete all their people from social media, their friends, relatives, etc., so that your ex cannot keep tabs on you via them.

If your ex, who dumped you, doesn't initiate contact after 2-4 weeks, they are most likely not missing you enough and believe they have made the right decision to break up. They have disqualified themselves because they are not interested in you. Remember, you are using the No Contact rule because your partner/love interest broke up with you.

Therefore, it wouldn't make sense to continue contact or initiate contact after some time.

So, to simplify it, here are the rules in bullet points for easy reference:

The general rule at a glance:

- Don't call, message, or engage with your ex's social media anymore.

- Unfriend and unfollow them and go on a complete social media detox.
- Don't go to places where you'd have an "accidental" encounter with them.
- Don't wish them happy Birthday, Valentine's, Easter, Christmas, Thanksgiving, etc.
- Don't express your condolences if they lose a family member or a friend.
- Hide every reminder of them that's within your control.
- Avoid going to places that can potentially elicit painful memories.

Mutual Friends

- Cut mutual friends out of your life until you've moved on, or at least distance yourself from them.
- Don't hang out with them just to please them.
- Cut out those who contribute to drama between you and your ex.
- Instruct your friends not to come to you with any updates about your ex.
- Avoid fishing for information, be it directly or indirectly.
- Don't have uncomfortable ex-related conversations, and don't be shy about asking your friends to change the topic.
- If your friendships enable you to maintain any sort of connection to your ex, you're breaking no contact and should stop immediately.

Your ex's Family

- If you're close with your ex's family, let them know that you'll be out of touch for a while.
- If they ask for reasons you are distancing from them, just tell them you're hurting and need time to heal.
- Don't stress if they reach out. They may still be a bit attached to you and are struggling with the breakup, too - but also remember, they are your ex's family; they have your ex's back, not yours.
- Don't ask your ex's family members to pass information about them to you or vice versa.

Handling Belongings

- Ask a friend to retrieve your stuff and get them to hand your ex back their stuff if you have any.

"Is it true that if you don't contact your ex after a breakup, they'll return to you?"

Whether the ex comes back depends solely on whether they still have feelings for you, and you need to remember that it is out of your control.

Here are a few scenarios that can happen:

First scenario

Your ex decides to break up with you, and then this happens ….

- *You took the time to talk with them about why it no longer worked out.*
- *They ask that you not contact them because they need time on their own to think things through.*
- *You accepted their decision to split, even though you love them and miss them.*
- *You accepted moving on in life without them.*
- *You never thought about getting back with them as you respected their decision.*
- *You decided to focus on yourself, your personal development, your personal growth, and better still ... your life.*
- *You made yourself a top priority, not your ex.*
- *As time went by, you detached yourself even if there was still love and affection.*
- *They got curious, wondering what you were doing because you didn't contact them; they are scared they have lost you for good and realise the mistake they made.*
- *They contact you.*

Second scenario

Your ex dumped you for whatever reason. Maybe it was your fault, maybe theirs and:

- *During the No Contact rule, you didn't focus on how YOU were feeling on improving yourself and your life situation.*
- *You were needy and insecure, focused on what THEY might be doing, if they met someone else, etc.*

- *You were afraid that the silence was them thinking you didn't care or that they would forget you and move on.*
- *You contacted them out of neediness, just to find out that they are happy without you and out of fear.*
- *Maybe they already met someone else, which is a sign they left the relationship a long time ago. Even if they didn't meet someone, they still don't have intentions of getting back with you.*

Third scenario

- *You both break up and don't keep in contact.*
- *You might still miss them or not; they might still miss you or not.*
- *Maybe both of you miss each other, maybe you don't.*
- *You have no intention of getting back with them and don't ask yourself if they feel the same.*
- *You don't reach out to see how they are doing, maybe out of indifference, maybe out of worry of bothering them. It might be vice versa for them.*

Fourth scenario

- *After the breakup, you are doing great after a few months of not communicating with them.*
- *You made so much progress, living life on your own terms and accomplishing great things.*
- *You have learned to be self-reliant and improve in many areas of your life.*

- *You contact your ex, or maybe they contact you.*
- *You are not playing games or using strategies to get back; you are just being honest with your feelings, no matter the outcome.*
- *Maybe you guys get back together, maybe you just stay friends, or maybe you lose contact for years and the rest of your lives.*

These scenarios, and many others, happen after no contact. Sometimes, people get back together because they still have feelings; sometimes, they don't because it is officially over and can never be restored to how it was. I know that for me, no contact didn't always mean I wanted to get back with an ex and vice versa. Sometimes, it was just over.

Also, no contact is lived differently according to

- *whether or not you were the dumper or the dumpee,*
- *if you are a man or a woman,*
- *your age,*
- *and if the breakup was messy or amicable.*

Was the breakup messy or amicable? If it was messy, where you might have been responsible, apologise for your part in it, and accept to give them space and time. If they were the culprit and their reasons seem selfish, mean, heartless, untrustworthy, or superficial, or they have a life situation that you cannot tolerate, don't try to win them back with no contact; sever ties permanently! You deserve so much better!

Once you understand the reason behind the breakup and everything is explained, you go to No Contact. During this time, try not to focus on whether they will contact you or not or what they may or may not be doing at any given time. It may make you feel worse initially and even take a week or two to get your head around this, and that's fine.

In this time, you focus on yourself, your healing, and your own personal well-being. This is a time to detach yourself totally from your ex. It is going to be hard for the first month, so you must take things one day at a time. Feel the pain, cry, feel sorry for yourself, watch Netflix, eat ice cream, and have a massive pity party. It is okay to live with all the honest emotions you go through, and you need to go through it to get over it.

After that, you are going to start journaling in a notebook. Yup, you heard that right!

Trust me when I tell you that journaling during No Contact works wonders. It empties out all the negative emotions you are carrying. These can be reasons why you miss your ex and how it makes you feel anxious, insecure, and weak. Write down those emotions and feel them. It is a grieving process that you cannot avoid.

I have created a 30-day journal to aid in this journey through the first 30 days of No Contact. It has motivational daily quotes, guides you to write your feelings down daily, and provides you with support. It is available on Amazon and is titled '30 Day No Contact

Journal', or don't forget; you can simply use a notepad you have at home. However, you do it; get writing!

CHAPTER 4

"How to move forward whilst in no contact".

May I suggest that should you find yourself reminiscing about your ex, you try to think of the times you were not happy in the relationship and the flaws of your ex?

This is not to drag your ex through the mud or paint them black. It's just a reminder that your ex and your relationship were not perfect and had flaws and faults, too. No relationship in history ended because it was so great.

So, stop looking at the past relationship through rose-tinted glasses and take them right off that pedestal. Then, with your newly acquired free time, see the advantages of the freedom you have now, things you couldn't do when you were with them as it would have caused problems. Also, write down weekly goals you wish to achieve. Focusing on those goals and self-development during No Contact is very beneficial.

Now, ask yourself what you would like to accomplish three months from now. And don't just say, "Getting back with my ex." This should be something that will improve your life and add to your personal development. It could be on an academic level, your career, your health, becoming a better person, learning a new language or an instrument, travelling, etc.

Nevertheless, I think exercise should be on that list. Getting in shape for the next three months will make you feel better, have more energy, and look so much better. It could be in the gym, at home, or outdoors. Heck, just walking an hour while listening to a podcast or your music at full blast (no love songs) can make you feel better.

Reading books instead of watching TV can also help your mental development, motivate you to be more confident and proactive, and make you less anxious, insecure, and needy. Don't stay home; go and see places, do some volunteer work, or visit friends & family.

Now, here's the thing: while you're doing things to improve yourself and the quality of your life, getting better every day without your ex, perhaps they'll contact you after a month, two months, three months, or maybe never again. If that's the case, you are better off now, even if you might miss them. However, if they do contact you, don't just take them back right away. I repeat, DON'T just take them back right away. The fact is you should probably ask yourself how it will benefit you to take them back.

I know it's tempting to want to rush back into their arms if your ex should come knocking ... but hear me out. You've been working so hard on yourself, growing, and blossoming into this amazing person who deserves the world. Why would you want to jeopardise all that progress for someone who couldn't see your value before?

Take a step back and truly think about what taking them back would mean for you.

- *Are the issues that caused the split resolved?*
- *Are they genuinely a changed person who will cherish you this time around?*
- *Do they have another motive to reconcile?*
- *Or are they just feeling a bit lonely and nostalgic, looking for a familiar comfort?*

You owe it to yourself to be discerning. If they do reach out, don't be afraid to lay out your boundaries and expectations. You're not the same person they walked away from.

Only consider letting them back in if they can prove they've done the work, too, and are truly committed to your happiness and growth as a couple. At the end of the day, trust your gut. If reconciling doesn't feel right deep down, don't force it. If this isn't right, you'll be back at square one when they break up with you again. You're thriving without them, and there could be an even better love story waiting for you down the line.

Take your time.

Remember, no contact should be used to detach yourself from your ex. This doesn't mean you don't care about them and that your relationship was not worth it. It just means detaching yourself so you find your self-worth again, that you can:

- *stand on your two feet,*
- *grow,*

- *evolve,*
- *adapt,*
- *grow strong.*

and you did all of this on your own!!

If your former partner contacts or doesn't contact you, it is their doing and has nothing to do with your worthiness. Also, after a few months, if you do not contact them for the right reasons, you will work out how you feel, and you will see things for how they really were, and you will start feeling better after 2 months and even better after 3 months, and so on.

"What do dumpers feel during no contact?"

Initially, your ex might feel a sense of relief, like a weight has been lifted off their shoulders. They've probably been mulling over this decision for a while, even if the breakup caught you off guard.

They may be out there revelling in their newfound freedom, enjoying life without you by their side. And that's precisely why going radio silence during this period is crucial. Any attempt at contact from you will likely be met with a cold shoulder or, worse, push them even further away.

Whilst breakups are brutal, the urge to reach out to your ex may get strong. But right now, it is not the best idea. They need space to process this split and rediscover who they are without you. And you, my darling, need time to heal your heart and focus on your fabulous self.

After a month or two, your ex may have even dated again and realised that this new person lacks the qualities that you had. They will weigh the pros and cons of being in a new relationship and may even end it. These are called rebound relationships, and that's why it's never a good idea to date someone who is fresh out of another relationship. You will always be compared to the ex!

By this time, your ex will realise you are not blowing up their phone, begging to be taken back. This piques their curiosity about the reason behind this behaviour. They may then wonder what you are up to and start checking your social media, unblocking you if they have blocked you, and generally take actions that alert you to the fact that they are thinking about you curiously. I literally Hear this day I my Breakup Coaching sessions. In such a situation, you should not respond at all.

Even if they send messages like "Hi, how are you?" or" Miss you," you should either ignore those messages or respond in a brief, fun, easy-going way and then disengage. Never … and I mean NEVER, respond instantly like an excited puppy! So many people make this mistake (so make sure you don't).

Having stuck out No Contact to this stage, some people respond in a way that indicates they are super excited that their ex is coming back into their life, and they reply, "Oh my, I have missed you'" or "It has made my day to hear from you, can we meet up to talk?". These kinds of responses show the dumper that they don't have to act on their curiosity right now because you are right there where they left you, dangling on a string …. and all your hard work of No Contact will have been undone in that split second.

Don't worry if you think that by not rushing in to reply, your ex will think you're not interested. That's the WHOLE point of no contact: to make your ex think you're not interested, to show them that you have accepted their decision and are fine and can live your life without them. That makes you high value in their eyes and, therefore, more likely to feel that they need to up their game to catch your attention. You suddenly become the prize again … the tables turn!

Usually, after about four months, if your ex is going to reach out to you to talk to you about getting back together, it will happen about that time. If you don't hear from them in four months, it probably isn't going to happen. Not to say it will NEVER happen. One of my exes came back to me after three years of no contact!

So, to reiterate, it is likely that your ex will be confident and happy just after they have initiated the breakup, while you will be sad and confused. But if you go no contact and focus on yourself, then in time, YOU will become confident and happy, and your ex will be confused and uncertain. This transition almost always happens. It doesn't always lead to exes coming back, but they will almost certainly be checking up on you after 2 or 3 months if you leave them alone, and you don't have to do anything.

CHAPTER 5

"The possibility of breaking no contact".

If the No Contact rule is too hard and you want to contact your ex (I do not recommend this), I suggest waiting at least 60 days before considering contacting them again.

However, you must prepare yourself. Some exes may get back together, while others don't. If your ex no longer has romantic feelings for you or they meet someone else, I can understand how painful this will be. But at least you can move on and find someone who loves you.

One Size Does Not Fit All ... There Are Exceptions to the Rule

Firstly, let me advise you to trust no contact. It is the most effective method for getting an ex back as it allows them to truly experience the breakup and gives them a chance to miss you. It is even better for helping you heal the immense heartbreak that you are suffering, even though it does not feel like that at the time. Trust me. It really is the only way.

But come closer and listen up... If your ex is forced to experience the breakup and the loss of you in their lives instead of you constantly contacting them trying to get them back, as I have already mentioned, your ex can feel the loss of you and realise that he or she does not want the breakup.

It is also the mature adult response when someone wants to go their separate way. Trying to force yourself back into their life is not mature and comes across as desperate and needy. And my darling, you do NOT want to appear immature, needy, or desperate – it's not attractive in any language.

So, trust no contact even though it is bloody hard!

Scenarios When You Could Break No Contact

Don't see this next part as a loophole so you can reach out to your ex. When you are heartbroken, it will temporarily make you feel better to speak with them, but in doing so, you risk pushing your ex further away, making a reunion less likely. Let me give you some examples of when you should not use the No Contact rule or when you could temporarily break it (only if you want your ex back; if you do not, then skip to the next part).

1. If Your Ex Reaches Out to You First

I've heard many other people online say that when you're No Contact, and your ex who dumped you contacts you, you should never respond!

Let me tell you, I have been on the phone with so many clients who have done this, and it went something like this:

- *Their ex reached out to them.*
- *They ignored their ex.*
- *Their ex reached out again.*
- *They ignored their ex.*
- *Their ex never reached out again.*

Let me ask you something: Why would your ex reach out yet again if he or she thinks you're just going to ignore them forever? Who could deal with that level of rejection? Who would want to feel that embarrassment? Pride could stop them from continuing to reach out.

If you put your ex in that position, they will assume that you do not want to talk to them, that you are over them, and they will stop trying to talk to you simply because they believe that you won't respond anyway and that you are done with them and their pride will stop them contacting again, even if they wanted to.

So, if you are healing nicely and do not want them back anymore, or you want to ignore your ex, you certainly can, but I don't recommend it if you want your ex back. Ignoring them if they call/text you will just cause them to go away permanently when you might have had a chance of reuniting.

I have too much experience in the school of hard knocks to recommend that. If your ex reaches out to you, I'm not suggesting that you get too excited; start screaming with excitement and start telling them how much you have missed them and want them back. No, No, and thrice No!!

I'm just suggesting that you calmly reply to them so that they see you won't just ignore them. You don't have to, and shouldn't, take control of the conversation. They need to try at this stage so you can see their motive in contacting you (sometimes, it can just be for an ego stroke). If you're acting too keen at this stage, this could scare them off; they need to see that you can live without them... It makes them question if they can live without you!

If your ex is sending lame messages that aren't worth replying to, e.g., "What was the name of that Salmon dish that you cooked for my mum that time?" or "Did I leave a green sock at yours?" then 100% ignore them. They need to make more effort. So, if they just send a random weak message, that's likely to be an 'ego' reach out, and when you reply, it could leave you feeling worse than you were.

So, to clarify, my definition of no contact does not include ignoring your ex if they reach out to you (Just make sure it is a text worth replying to) It just means that you never initiate contact with them first.

2. If You Have Children, Property, or Business Together

One of the more obvious times when you can't use a full, strict form of No Contact is when you have children with your ex. This is also the case if you own a home, property, or a business with them. You have no choice but to speak with them occasionally, so you must go into a watered-down version of No Contact … Limited Contact.

I understand the challenges of maintaining a healthy co-parenting relationship after a breakup. Having children together means you can't completely cut off contact, so a limited contact approach is necessary. The key is to keep interactions strictly focused on matters related to the children and avoid any unnecessary communication or small talk. It's important to prioritise the well-being of your children above all else.

This means setting aside personal differences and committing to being the best co-parents you can be. Communicate respectfully and objectively when discussing parenting matters, schedules, or any issues involving the kids. At the same time, be mindful of not overstepping boundaries or engaging in conversations that veer into personal territory.

It can be tempting to reach out for non-essential reasons as you may miss your ex but resist that urge. Limit your interactions to only what is necessary for the children's sake. Remember, your goal is to provide a stable and healthy environment for your kids, even if it means having to maintain a cordial, business-like relationship with your ex. With time and consistency, this limited contact approach can help your ex to realise what they have lost.

You might miss your ex, and it may make you feel good to speak to them, so you might find yourself deliberately creating an issue related to your children to justify reaching out to them. However, you only hurt yourself by doing that because the less contact you have with your ex, the higher the chance that they will miss you and see that they don't want to be apart from you (if you wish to reconcile).

I really do understand that talking to your ex could make you feel better and that right now, you might feel desolate not having them in your life. But if you want them back, they need to realise that they miss you … and you simply cannot miss someone who is always there for you.

So, if you have property or business with them, again, keep in contact ONLY with necessary, important issues. If possible, avoid all contact completely. Also, if there is another way it can be handled with a third party or by you, go for that option every time.

So, to reiterate, if you are practising no contact when you have children together, exceptions will need to be made.

"What if you work together or own a property together?"

Alright, let's get real about working with an ex. It's a tricky situation where maintaining no contact is nearly impossible. In such cases, you must adopt what I call "limited contact." Limited contact is essentially the same as the No Contact rule but with a few tweaks. The differences come into play when you're forced to interact with your ex due to work obligations.

Let's say that you are working with your ex at a pickle factory. They come over and say, "Hey, I need you to order more vinegar." You should respond professionally and order the vinegar without engaging in personal conversations. The No Contact rule aims to create space and allow emotions to settle, not to alienate your ex in a mean way. Remember, the goal is to potentially reconcile, not to burn bridges or create resentment.

You want to minimise the conversation with them, keeping it strictly about business. If they turn the conversation to your relationship, give a one-word answer. How you deliver this one-word answer is crucial. If they say, "Hey, do you remember that time we went on a jet ski, and it broke down in the ocean?" Don't say, "Yes, I remember that time! That was so scary!" Simply look nonchalant and say, "Yes." It's just one word.

They will not know how to react to that. It will put them in a position where they think, "Something is off." It's almost like they won't know how to perceive you. No one reacts that way. Concise yet succinct responses are essential.

Those are my top tips for using the limited No Contact rule at work. With limited contact at work, you want to avoid conversation as much as you can. If you're forced to talk to your ex, that's okay. Keep it strictly about business. If they bring up your relationship at all, one-word answers are great. The way you say the one-word answer is important.

I realise I wasn't specific when I said, "Keep it strictly about business." Let's go back to the pickle factory example, and your ex is your boss or colleague. They tell you, "I need you to fill up the pickle jars." You can look at them and say, "Okay, I'll do that." It's strictly business. If they bring up a business-related task like counting money or clearing the counters, you just remain very nice and polite.

This is also the case if you own a home, property, or a business with them. You have no choice but to communicate with them occasionally, so you must adopt a limited contact approach.

CHAPTER 6

"We value that which does not come easy to us".

Some Breakup Coaches will say that when you do No Contact, it is permanent and that you should never, under any circumstances, reach out to your ex ever again.

So, whilst I do recommend never reaching out if they dumped you, I also understand the basic reasoning behind these instructions; the fact is that if getting your ex-back is all that you want and desire, I've got nearly three decades of extremely hard-earned wisdom & experience that gazumps that ideology.

In my own experiences and in talking to my clients, I have noticed that after 6 weeks, the odds drop dramatically that your ex will reach out to you. The odds increase that your ex will move on completely and that they could find somebody else (not in all cases, but the odds change)

Initially, they may just be rebounding, but the more time that has passed by, the more the relationship your ex might get into is more likely to be something more serious than that.

The bottom line is:

After 60 days, it is more unlikely that you will hear from your ex again, so if you are not over them and you want them back for all the right reasons, you have nothing to lose by reaching out to them first. The main reason I say that it is more justified to reach out after enough time has passed is because you don't want to live your life wondering what if.

For example, I speak to many people who do the dumping. I know that this may come as a surprise to some of you since I am generally writing this for those who have been dumped, but people who do the dumping often book coaching sessions with me to help get their ex back. They realise that they have made a huge mistake but do not know how to rectify it. They mostly realise when their ex is not contacting them (more proof that no-contact works!)

That's right. It's not always clear to them how to get their ex back. Many times, they are scared, petrified, in fact!

They don't know what they would say or if you'll even want to speak with them. I tell them that it is time to put their big pants on and initiate that contact, as it was their decision to end the relationship in the first place. It might surprise you how much time I must spend convincing them that they should reach out because they feel sick and anxious at the thought of rejection.

I will be honest, though; this really does not apply to most people who initiate breaking up. Most of the time, the dumper knows that if they want to get back together, they must be the ones to reach out, but sometimes they don't know what to do and feel extremely anxious about it.

I'm not telling you this so that you'll break no-contact and reach out to your ex in hopes that they have been wanting to reach out but didn't know how or were too scared to do so. Don't use that as an excuse! At least, not until enough time has passed without contact.

"How Much Time is Enough?"

Well, this is the million-dollar question! As a rule of thumb, I would say it's 60 days. If you hold out for that amount of time, you risk nothing (but a bit of pride) by reaching out to them.

Wondering 'what if?' is never good, so what do you have to lose? I've explained certain situations when you should not use the no-contact rule. When in doubt, default to not contacting your ex.

But before you reach out, ask yourself these questions first:

- *Do you feel confident in your true feelings about your ex?*
- *You know the circumstances of the breakup; would your ex want you back?*
- *Did something unforgivable cause your breakup (are you flogging a dead horse)?*
- *Are you willing to work on improving your relationship if you get back together?*
- *Did you miss them, or did you just miss having someone as a support system?*
- *Do you want your ex and what they bring to the table, or do you just not want the annoyance of starting again with a new relationship?*
- *Do you really want your ex, or do you just not like being alone?*

- *Do you want your ex back because you are having trouble meeting someone new?*

One rule of thumb is that if your ex is interested, wants to get back together, and misses you, they will reach out to you, seeing as they initiated the breakup. As I explained above, it's not 100% of the time, but it is most of the time.

I am so aware that each person's situation is different and that no contact is difficult but give it your best shot if you really want your ex back. If you do not get them back, at least you will have moved on with style and class, and my darling, who does not want to be stylish and classy?

CHAPTER 7

"Real-life accounts of how no contact worked out in practice".

"So, when I had my heart broken, I spent many hours trawling the Web looking for the real results of doing No-Contact. It made me feel less alone and gave me hope that I would not always feel this way. I have also spoken to many clients who did the same thing. Because of this, I decided to add some for you. These are all genuine and real, and I have permission to post them … It helped me, so I thought it may help you too".

Here are some real accounts of how using the no-contact method worked out for people who felt probably just as awful as you feel right now.

Sarah-Jane ~ 28

"So last week, I reached the 30-day no-contact mark after complete silence on both ends. I had very high hopes of feeling SO much better about our split after four weeks. Time went by without him in my life. I wasn't playing a game; I just stayed as busy as I could. I used my journal a lot, and that really helped me process my feelings of missing him.

But then, this put a spanner in the works: last week, he showed up at my friend's sandwich shop. She was polite to him, as usual, and he asked her about me. And began pleading his case about the breakup.

He told her he still loves me and thinks of me every day. I took this as him testing the waters, wanting some sort of contact with me and wanting me back and I was so happy (the first time I had smiled in ages). The following morning, I saw him at a coffee shop, though I'm not sure if he saw me. He was pulling up as I was getting into my car. After a month of not seeing his face, this hit me like a sledgehammer. I was shaking and began to cry whilst sitting in my car. Later that morning, my emotions got the better of me, and I texted him. I told him I saw him that morning, and I missed him. But no reply!! I could kick myself as it knocked me back to day one emotionally.

So, my point is, I don't know if you will hear from your ex again. But it's comforting to know, on some level, that, even if there's no contact, they are hurting just like you. If love was involved, I could be glad for that, even if he chose not to reply to me. I moved on and met the nicest guy in the world! He was far more compatible with me, and it made me realise why the other one did not work out.

If you are going through this just try to have faith that one day you will wake up, and it will just hurt a lot less. Hang in there. And think positively!

Marcus ~ 31

To put it bluntly, the only times I was successful in getting my exes back were when I was not trying to get them back. There was no big scheme; it was the fact that I accepted the reality of the situation and kept living my life without them in it.

When they left me, I respected their decisions, stayed calm and rational, and wished them well. Then, I used no contact,

not as a tactic to get them back but because I decided to live my life without them being part of my future. Because I showed nonchalance, detachment, and readiness to move on, they ran back to me.

When I did the opposite because I was insecure, overbearingly needy, and missed them, it never worked.

I am not suggesting you do this to win your ex back. When the relationship is over, and you decide to move on without them, the reasons they come back are because they still have feelings for you and realise they made a mistake. And then there are others when you move on without them, they do the same because they no longer have romantic feelings for you.

In my experience, it is better not to go back with an ex. In most cases, you will eventually break up again, as the issues that caused the break will likely still be there. If it has been a while since you have been together, go for it, but also be realistic.

Miley ~ 29

I broke no contact with my ex-boyfriend after 28 days.

28 days of going out with friends, working on myself, going to the gym, reflecting on the relationship, and trying to become a better person. On paper, I did everything I was meant to during no-contact. But for me, it was 28 days of pure hell. 28 days of questioning myself. 28 days of looking at my phone.

28 days of crying and wondering why and how. Wondering what he was doing. I always felt like there was meant to be more to our relationship. It was a TV show that at the end says, "To be continued......."

So, I broke contact.

I messaged him a few times and got basic amicable responses. I called him and told him we needed to meet as we still had each other's stuff. He was kind and considerate, and he agreed to meet.

When we met, I was able to lay out everything I had on my mind. I told him what I'd been getting up to during no contact. I told him how much I'd thought that I had let us and the relationship down. I was able to ask if he was happy right now. I told him that I felt our relationship still had more to it and didn't feel like it was meant to be over. I even put it to him that he felt this too. He didn't deny it but said his mind was made up. I asked if we could try again but take it very slowly. But the answer was no. He stuck to his guns.

However, it was exactly what I needed. What I needed to hear to be able to heal. I was brave and gave it one last shot. I put all my cards on the table. I got the questions that were burning my mind and keeping me awake answered. We parted ways. It was bittersweet. He said he still cares and still loves me. I told him I'd give him space as he said he couldn't talk to me anytime soon again as it was too hard for him. I told him I might touch base on his birthday to wish him a happy birthday. He didn't say no. So now I will just wait. I'll see what time brings. But for now, I'm at peace. Hopefully, in the future, my book will get another chapter. But not just yet.

So, if you're going to break no-contact, break it for you. Break it because you feel like you are going crazy and just can't do another day. Be ready to talk calmly and lay your heart out there for her. Be ready to take possible rejection, but you have nothing to lose.

Good luck."

Claudia - 32

The mad thing is that when I was super upset, I heard nothing, but the minute I went on with my life, my ex started to wonder what he lost.

I was devastated when we broke up and called him all the time. I did not give him any headspace to figure things out for himself, and by the time it was really and truly "over", I had about six months of begging & pleading with him behind me.

It got really tiring, and even though I knew I loved him, I couldn't make him want to be with me, marry me, or do all the things that it felt like we should be doing after so much time together. He just wasn't feeling the same as me.

So, I kept him in my life at a distance and went and enjoyed myself to the fullest. He likely saw me in a different light, I wasn't the same upset ex-girlfriend anymore but a friend with a full life and a potential new boyfriend.

I think the latter really jolted him into action. But yes, not contacting him and giving him space to think about things did help us find our way back to each other. We have now been married for three years and have a baby on the way.

I don't think it's a game; it's a way of life. If someone doesn't want to be with you, then you need to honour their request and move on with your own life. You may be pleasantly surprised. Perhaps a new relationship is on the horizon, the relationship you need to build with yourself. Take time to really understand yourself without someone else next to you.

Good luck. Breakups are hard, but they teach you (but not if you don't let them). And besides, who wants to get back together with someone who is begging, whining, and pleading? If nothing else, save your pride.

Tilly - 26

I think if a relationship is meant to be, it will be regardless, even if things end.

Years ago, I had an ex whom I was totally besotted with. He just slowed down contact with me out of the blue. He didn't actually finish with me or anything; he just became distant,

and I knew he didn't want me. Then he completely ghosted me. I was devastated and cried for months over it.

It slowly started to become easier and easier, but it was like he had a sixth sense, and he then suddenly became interested again. Now, bearing in mind that I was still hopelessly in love with him, he kept leading me into a false sense of security - never actually committing, making false promises, etc.- until the same thing happened.

Fast forward 2 years, and I've got him at my beck and call... I stopped contact and started seeing other people. Whenever he texted me, I'd say I couldn't see him or I was too busy, and he became more interested in me to the point he asked me to marry him, and I refused. I couldn't, as I just don't feel that way about him anymore. He is now just a friend, and I can't believe how I used to feel about him. He was so wrong for me, and it doesn't even seem real to me now.

I would say no-contact works, but it has to be more than just no-contact. You need to not think about him/her so much. Live your life, and before you know it, they will surely contact you... I've never had an ex not contact me at some point.

Good luck

Bill - 33

No contact isn't a method to get an ex back, and if you use it as such, you will be left bitterly disappointed.

No contact is the method that makes it easier for a person to move on from a broken shitty relationship.

It has a side effect in some cases of causing an ex who didn't want to break up to get in touch, which puts that ex in a weaker position because they're doing the chasing.

If your ex doesn't care and isn't interested, no contact won't change that, but it is the perfect way to find out someone's true feelings for you, and you can then meet someone worth your time.

Mia - 33

It was just amazingly wonderful. The minute I got him back, all previous issues were gone, and it was a fairy tale!!

Just kidding…

Unless you identify what went wrong with a relationship, you won't find out what areas of your life need improvement. Relationships are our mirrors.

Our heartbroken brains tell us that staying in contact with your ex will keep your relationship alive. Every time you call or text your ex, you advertise just how needy and desperate you are. This is where no contact comes in super handy!

My sage advice is to calm down and collect yourself emotionally after your breakup. That means no contact, no posting photos to get their attention, and no doing anything

that they may see.

They can't miss you if they don't know what losing you tastes like.

It is time to focus solely on yourself. Exercise, level up your diet, meditate, and educate yourself. But mostly, have fun in your relationship with yourself.

Playfulness and confidence attract people to you. Not only do you end up attracting your ex back, but you also match with people who match your vibes, so it is a win-win.

Connor - 36

If you are solely looking at 'No Contact' as a way of getting them back, you're just delaying the heartbreak and pain.

If they contact you and you want to get back to them, then lucky you. But you can't just sit by the phone waiting for them—there's a good chance that it will never ring.

Kain ~ 37

Actually, no contact should only be used so you can heal.

Take a step back and evaluate the situation.

Is your ex really worth it?

Did everything look good even without your rose-stained glasses (which in itself takes 1-2 months to take off, BTW) to move on and see if you'll find someone who will treat you and love you better? It takes at least 3 months to get over someone who had become more of a habit than love. So, take 3 months to focus on yourself and get better in every way, find new people, and there is a 70% chance by the end of it, you'll be completely over your ex and be ready to move on to someone better suited.

If not, you can both, very maturely, being well informed now of where you stand, reach out and see if you want to try again and all the things you thought an issue, and they thought was an issue during these 3 months of no contact (with freedoms from influence from this person) should be brought to the table and discussed or you're headed down the same rabbit hole. Either way, no contact is a conscious way to break the habit of having them in our lives. If you keep them in your mind or in your future, even if you get back, history will repeat itself.

3 months NO CONTACT IS TO GET OVER SOMEONE, not get back with someone.

Jack - 33

I broke up with my ex-girlfriend after I felt she violated my trust. A few months later, I asked her to come back to me because I'd forgiven her, but she declined.

I said OK and never bothered her again after that.

Eight months later, she contacts me, saying she misses me and asking me to hang out. At this point, I'd already had a new girlfriend and was very happy, so I declined.

Funny. Seems like life gives you what you want when you stop wanting it.

Willow - 34

The key to this is to redirect your focus from obsessive compulsion over your ex to applying self-care. The best revenge is getting yourself to a place where you no longer care about revenge.

Stabilise your mind. Identify your limiting beliefs like "I am not worthy of a healthy relationship" or "People cheat, I will never get a person to commit to me" What you believe, you promote in your life. When you accept your fears, you get to live them daily. Realise that the failed relationship was here to teach you a lesson and set new higher standards.

Raising your self-esteem and prioritising alone time changes what you want from a relationship. The blessing of changing your mindset is that you no longer want your ex back, and you get a chance to meet your real soul mate.

You are welcome.

Stan - 28

The real purpose of the 'no contact' rule is to understand whether the other person cares for you or not i.e., to know where you stand in their life.

Give your ex all the space in the world to miss you, and then will get your answer!

And for you to find out what you really want and if your ex was able to give you that

There are no guarantees that the ex will come back if you use the no-contact rule. I feel you should have done more good than bad for your ex to come back. And there should be some attraction left in order for them to contact you. The best thing is to consider it over and move on. If they come back, it's good. If they don't, then just think that they had a purpose in your life, and that purpose has been fulfilled :)

Leo - 23

I got dumped for a guy with a Porsche and pots of cash who was 20 years older than her or me. I begged her to come back. I got nowhere but blocked and ignored.

So, I used the no-contact technique, and it took 2 1/2 months for her to call and say I made a mistake, I miss you, and I want your back.

But by then I had met the most amazing female I've ever run into. I've been spending days and nights at her house and have never felt this kind of chemistry or love in my life. I told the Ex I moved on. It hurts, but it's the right thing to do, as she left me and ripped my heart out. Finding the new love made me wake up to the fact that I was chasing the idea of loving her, and I'm not in love with her anymore.

It's the hardest thing I've been through. What I was told was, "Take a long, deep breath and let a cool breeze blow through you, then focus your energy where it's most needed and start making yourself better. Ignore the Ex and truly follow the rules of no contact, and I promise she will at least call to see how you are. But by the time a few months go by and the no-contact rule is at its most powerful, you may not even want them back. Good luck.

Tamara - 45

It is so annoying! People always get this strategy wrong! It's NOT manipulative.

It's NOT a game, and most importantly, It's NOT intended to get your ex back! No contact is not the reason that brings someone back, it's just the consequence of what might happen if you do go no contact.

So, what is no contact? It's a technique for YOU to use to move on with some self-respect. It's to get you back to being happy and loving life again without the need for *your ex to provide you with that happiness.*

Obviously, when you were begging like a fool, that wasn't working, am I right? It wasn't working because you were operating on selfish motives and fuelled with fear & high anxiety. It wasn't working because your ex was feeling the neediness from you, and that made them run for the hills.

No contact gives them time and space from you so they can work on themselves as well. It allows them to think about you in a rational way again.

I feel that to really change who we are, it takes months, not weeks. Changing old habits takes a lot of self-reflection. After a few months go by and they haven't heard from you, they start to wonder about you, and that is why there is always that possibility for them to come back.

For me, I've done no contact in order to move on, not to get them back and both guys did reach out to check up on me after months of no contact. Nothing materialised romantically after contact, as I'm now dating someone totally amazing anyway, but what happens is that they were just curious about me or lonely and reached out.

It further improved my happiness. Knowing that they thought of me and reached out gave me a weird peace of mind (ego-related?).

Harry - 26

I went no contact for two weeks, and then I got weak with one

message. Now I'm on day 12. I feel good. She can contact me at any time on any platform. I, however, have cleansed her from my flat and my phone, so I don't see what she's up to.

It's not the first time I've used no contact with the same person. As soon as I stop, she starts getting curious.

In fact, I've done it that many times, it's easy. The first time I did, it was hard. I put the work into me though, so now it's easier. Yes, I do miss her, and yes, I could easily contact her. I learned to be disciplined, and I now never get the urge to.

I focus on myself. I work hard, listen to new music, take my dog out for a couple of hours, and see my friends. In fact, I can't do all these things in one day, so throughout the week, I have always got something to do.

Trust me, my friend, the very moment you block, delete, and stop communicating, it gets easier day by day. All the articles you read are true. Give it 30 days, and you will feel 100 times better. I write down the date and time and have it on my fridge.

It's been 12 days for me. I feel better now than I did 12 days ago.

Challenge yourself, I dare you!

Betty - 29

In my case, the no-contact rule did not help me get my ex

back, but it helped me get myself back.

When my ex-boyfriend broke up with me, I was devastated. That night, I started searching online for advice on how to get an ex back. I came across the no-contact rule, and I decided to try it.

For about a month into no-contact, I was convinced that I was going to get my ex back. I missed him so much that he was all I wanted. He was the only person on my mind. After 2 months, my mindset completely changed. I realised that I'm better off without him and I am free from that heartache.

During the two months, I got to see his true colours which for me was a huge turn-off.

During this time, I also found myself. I put myself above everything else. I was determined to make the best out of this negative situation (it sounds corny, but it's true) and found the girl lost inside of me. When you are in a relationship, you can lose sight of who you are over time, especially if you put them first all the time.

But now I can say that I still don't want him back, and I'm so happy and pleased with the woman I am now.

So, I can definitely say that the no-contact rule was successful in giving me clarity. I hope my story can help whoever is reading this. You may want the person back right now, but turn that focus on yourself, and you will find clarity.

Deana - 46

If I close my eyes, I can still picture my sad self, feeling defeated and played for a fool yet again, heartbroken with tears falling as if someone had died. I know the date, time, and exactly what I was wearing.

My best friend was my rock, but she finally said, "BLOCK HIM. HE TAKES ANOTHER PIECE OF YOUR HEART EVERY TIME HE TREATS YOU THIS WAY!!!"

And the truth is she was right. My heart was broken into a million trillion pieces …

At that very moment, I impulsively blocked him on everything. To this day, I have never unblocked him, looked him up, stalked him, or contacted him again, and I never will.

I vanished, with no warning, after he hurt me and bruised my soul yet again.

Each time, it hurt more, not less, as you'd think I would have seen it coming, and it wouldn't have hurt so bad. That is not the case for me. The pain was gut-wrenching.

Even though I was a 44-year-old grown-up woman, I was still a naive, gullible, magic thinker with the heart and emotions of a little girl. I lived my life with blind faith and high hopes, still a believer in love and pure hearts despite the pain I've endured.

I used to hope & pray for him to contact me to validate that he didn't forget about me and that I meant something to him, but that has dissipated.

Damn, but yeah, those first days/weeks after I blocked him were the hardest for me because I knew it was final.

I am at peace now 💕

Mia - 34

It did work for me but not in the way you like it. It literally worked for ME.

Once upon a fairy-tale time, I fell in love (or so I thought). I had just gotten out of a bad marriage and after three years break, I started dating. I met this guy through Facebook. Send me a request, and it started from there. I was overwhelmed, to say the least, because, at 38, I was still desirable.

He was younger than me. He showered me with so much attention, chatted, called, and seemed so caring. I was swept completely off my feet. Then I got crazy with him. He felt pressured. Then, he just wanted a causal relationship—you know, the hook-up—or FWB. I declined. He broke up with me. My heart was shattered. I was literally down on the floor.

So, I searched online for ways to get back with an ex. I came up with this no-contact rule. I tried to use it with all my willpower. It was hard at first, but I was determined to do it just to get him back.

The first two weeks were super hard. Then, eventually, I got used to not contacting him. There was still radio silence on his side. In the third and fourth weeks, I began to stop stalking him. Taking a break from him gave me the time to think about the truth about us. I was not in a daze anymore; I could think more logically. I used those days to evaluate the relationship, myself, and my situation with him.

In the 6th week, he started sending me messages. I was so beyond tempted to reply to him, but I said to myself, no. In the 7th to 8th weeks, I was already over it and recovered. I came to my senses. Mia was back in the building!

He texted and called, begging to get me back and promising the world. But I said to myself, enough. I then decided to reply. He was happy. He said he wanted me back so badly.

My answer: "No, you don't want me. YOU JUST WANT A BONK!" (Oh my, if my dead grandmother read that text, she would die again!) And blocked him completely. It felt SOOO good! So yeah! It worked for me. Not with the result that I had in mind when I started ... but in a better way.

I didn't get him back.

I got myself back!

CHAPTER 8

"Conclusion"

My darling reader,

I understand how heartbreaking it can be to go through a breakup. It feels like the world is crashing down around you, and the pain seems unbearable. But trust me when I say there is light at the end of the tunnel. The sooner you gather the strength to let go and cut ties with your ex, the quicker you'll be able to heal those wounds and emerge as a stronger, wiser version of yourself. Silence really is your superpower!

Life goes on. One day soon, you'll find yourself having a gut-busting laugh over something utterly stupid, and you'll think to yourself, "I'm getting better." Finally, you'll know you're on the road to recovery.

Be kind to yourself. Be forgiving of yourself. And most of all, remember that being happily single is an alternative. Even if society is telling you that you must have a mate, take some time to heal before going back out there.

There are plenty of good people to love, but don't go back out there broken, jaded about love, etc. Accept reality. Experience the pain. Learn the lesson. Actively try to heal. Remember the person you were when you first met your ex and get that person back.

This experience, as painful as it may be, is an opportunity for growth. Take some time to reflect on what went wrong and be honest with yourself about the areas where you can improve yourself.

Embed those lessons deep within your heart and use them as a guide for your future relationships. You simply cannot lose on an investment in yourself.

Once you've done the work, it's there forever. And you can share it with whoever is lucky enough to end up with you. Be the best you that you can be ...

And the universe will take care of the rest.

Kel x

Keep in Touch

I would love to hear how you are doing. Please feel free to email me and let me know how you got on with No Contact.

Also, if you need more guidance and advice to help you navigate your breakup, check out my guided journal on Amazon, **'Bossing Your Breakup'**.

You can find me at www.kelscoaching.com. We can book a personal one-on-one coaching session; we talk about everything, nothing is off the table. Together, we are a force to be reckoned with, and you are not alone.

Printed in Great Britain
by Amazon

46103705R00056